CARDIFF Yesterday

D1523554

1 View of Cardiff looking south from the Castle Clock Tower, c.1871. Womanby Street is in the foreground, while in the centre is Cardiff Arms Park as it was before any building had been erected on the west side of Westgate Street. Beyond the Park are Temperance Town, the Railway Station, and the industrial training ship, *Havannah*.

Stewart Williams'
CARDIFF
Yesterday
Book Three

Foreword by
Dannie Abse

STEWART WILLIAMS

BARRY

First published in September, 1981

© Stewart Williams, Publishers,
Bryn Awel, Buttrills Road,
Barry, South Glamorgan

ISBN 0 900807 46 6

ACKNOWLEDGEMENTS

Warm thanks are extended to the following for kindly granting us permission to reproduce their photographs:

D. Affley (62, 161, 165); Peter Arch (55, 59); A. B. Ball (113, 114, 151); Bill Barrett (140, 164); T. J. Bodger (134, 137); Brian Canning (75, 76); Cardiff Central Library (1, 4, 7, 8, 14, 16, 17, 18, 29, 31, 34, 35, 38, 39, 40, 41, 48, 53, 54, 56, 65, 71, 77, 78, 80, 94, 96, 100, 138, 139, 186, 194, 196, 197, 202, 203, 206, 207, 214); J. Coombes (167); W. Coombes (99, 183); Angelo Corsi (126, 127, 128, 129); M. Crimmins (135); C. Crocker (163); Mrs J. E. Crowley (69, 204); Mrs P. Daly (87, 108, 174, 175, 177); I. V. Davies (144, 212); Tommy Davies (20, 30, 52, 57, 58, 61, 115, 148, 180, 182, 191); Howard Evans (122, 130, 132, 155, 157); Mrs V. J. Ferrissey (32, 106, 109, 110, 120, 141); Frank Goddard (123, 218); Arthur Granville (154); Mrs Jeanette Groves (116, 117, 211, 213); Mrs. N. Guildford (118); Victor Hardacre (209, 210); Tony Harrhy (119, 176); John Hill (168); G. James (70); Mrs P. James (112, 124, 125, 149, 217); S. James (88, 98, 111, 136); D. Jenkins (2, 3, 5, 6, 15, 19, 89, 90, 91, 92); Fred Jones (9, 10, 11, 13, 21, 22, 23, 24, 25, 26, 27, 28, 33, 37, 42, 43, 44, 45, 46, 47, 49, 50, 51, 63, 64, 66, 67, 68, 72, 73, 74, 79, 83, 93, 95, 97, 101, 102, 103, 142, 143, 145, 146, 147, 159, 160, 178, 179, 187, 188, 192, 193, 195, 198, 199, 200, 201, 205, 215, 216); Mrs P. Jones (104); T. Jones (158, 162); Doug Kestrell (169, 170, 171, 172); Mrs A. McIntyre (156); E. Mathews (189); Mrs Victoria Miller (173); Terry O'Connell (60, 85, 86); Dennis and Billy O'Neill (81, 82, 84, 131, 133); Spencer Powell (36); Jeff Price (190); H. B. Priestley (12, 208); J. K. Reypert (105); C. Steele (107, 152); Mrs A. Stubbs (121); Chris Taylor (181, 184, 185); N. Taylor (166); John Thomas (150); Mrs N. Wilson (153)

Printed in Wales by D. Brown & Sons Ltd., Cowbridge and Bridgend, Glamorgan

Return Ticket to Cardiff

by Dannie Abse

We were wandering Welsh Jews. I was born in Whitchurch Road, Cardiff, but after a year or two we were on the move. To 289 Albany Road, Cardiff. A few years later the wanderlust possessed my parents again and we shifted three minutes away to 237 Albany Road. A few years of stability and doors slamming before we trekked another five hundred yards to 66 Albany Road.

Was this an advance? We were nearer to the Globe Cinema now, where for 4d on a Saturday morning I could watch Tom Mix or Rin Tin Tin from the classy balcony and gob down on the kids who'd paid only 2d in the stalls. But my parents remembered the good old days at 289 Albany Road so, soon, we made Pickfords happy and moved back threequarters of a mile in that direction to 66 Sandringham Road. 'Sixty six is our lucky number,' my father said doubtfully.

Why did we move so frequently from rented house to house? Because the bathroom needed redecorating and had begun to look like a grudge; because though the jokes remained the same, my father's fortunes changed; because the mice had taken to chewing aphrodisiacs; because of Dai or Ken or Cohen the Crooner—for truly, sometimes, it is easier to move house than to get rid of certain guests.

I liked Cardiff. Until I was 18 all that I felt attracted to, all that I loved was circumscribed by its boundaries. Yet I must have had some curiosity about other cities, other countries, for I recall asking my mother: 'Where does England begin?' She promptly pointed to a nearby convenient railway bridge that crossed over Newport Road: 'By there,' she said. Though she was 25 miles wrong I thought for years that this side of the bridge was Wales where dark-haired men were human-size, 5 feet 8½ inches like I am now, whereas eastward—'over there'—the wrong side of that significant bridge strode alien flaxen-haired Englishmen affected with pituitary trouble.

South of our district, too, lived dangerous giants of a sort. Why else was I not allowed to go beyond Splott to the docks? 'People get knifed in Tiger Bay,' my mother warned me. Frankly, it was none too safe north of Albany Road either, for Philip Griffiths lurked there ready to bash me simply because he was a year older than I was or because I preferred Eldorado ice cream to Walls, or because I considered J. C. Clay a better bowler than Verity. Worse, after dark, coming home that way I had to pass St Margaret's Church graveyard where ghosts, magnified amoebae, slipped their chains so that between lamp-posts I would have to run faster than my own long shadow.

No, west was best. The direction of a 2A tram to Victoria Park where 'Billy the Seal' swam in pond water that needed a wash and where nearby, in a house called 'Mon Repos' lived Margaret Williams who wore no knickers.

West is best. I'd go that way 'into town' when mitching from school so that I could hide in the echoing acoustics of the National Museum where I would stare for hours at the illuminated tanks of tropical fish or at the glass-eyed stuffed animals caught forever in petrified movement. West was the direction of pleasure. Summer holidays and occasional Sundays my father would drive us to the nearby grey sullen sea of Penarth or Cold Knap or Ogmore-by-Sea or Porthcawl. Or back to where my mother was born—Ystalyfera—where she would converse in Welsh while the rest of us would listen without passports.

West was also the direction of religion. For I would have to travel that way to reach Windsor Place Synagogue and to that piece of holy ground near the secretive River Taff. That ground, where even tries were converted, was called Cardiff Arms Park, and there huge crowds would religiously sing *Land of My Fathers,* a national anthem that is half a dirge and half a battle cry.

I suppose most youngsters vacillate between fear and happiness. Midway is boredom. And boredom, too, is big on the map of Cardiff, for it is a rainy city where children press their noses against windowglass and whine, 'Mama, what shall I do now? What can I play now?' But when the sun is out, what a handsome city Cardiff is. When I return there now and loiter a bit—say at Roath Park Lake where I regularly swam as a boy until I got a duckshit rash—I am surprised how naturally beautiful are those places I once played in. I never realised this as a schoolboy. Few of us when young are enraptured by Nature as Wordsworth was. (Don't your children sitting in the back seat of the car—when you cry Look! Look! at a sunset or some dizzy vista—continue to quarrel or read their comics?) I certainly did not realise how charming are the corners of Cardiff.

But it's a long time ago now since, standing below Cardiff Castle, I was Robin Hood half way up the tower—which I remember one guide saying was built in the 16th century, oh aye, during Queen Victoria's reign. And it's a long time since I first stood on the terraces of Ninian Park when Cardiff City was bottom of Division 3 (South) and the brass band played 'Happy Days are Here Again' while I imagined myself to be their new signing about to change the soccer destiny of Wales.

Such triumphs would make 'them' put up a blue plaque for me like they did for Ivor Novello on that house he once occupied in Cowbridge Road. But they would have a problem. Which house would they choose? Would it be 289, 237 or 66 Albany Road? Or 66 Sandringham Road, or 66 Vaughan Avenue in Llandaff, or that house in Windermere Avenue half bombed during the war (while I was in it) or 198 Cathedral Road? (Cathedral Road was once the 'Arley Street of Cardiff, mun).

Well, since I'm dreaming why shouldn't I go the whole hog? Let them put blue plaques on the lot. Yes, so many blue plaques with the words: *Family Abse, wandering Welsh Jews, lived here.*

Part of an article published in Planet, August 1978, reproduced by permission of the author and with acknowledgements to the publisher.

AUTHOR'S NOTE

The success of *Cardiff Yesterday* owes much to the generous support it continues to receive. Dr Dannie Abse, the talented Cardiff-born poet and novelist, readily gave me permission to use the delightful piece which is printed above. His kindness is typical. From the outset I have had considerable help from Geoff Dart, County Librarian of South Glamorgan, whose constructive advice, based on years of accumulated knowledge, much of it unique, has illuminated many dark corners and added immeasurably to the quality of the books. Another good friend is Bill Barrett, popular headmaster of Gladstone School and indefatigable local historian, who has given me wholehearted backing and support. Fred Jones also deserves a special mention. Post cards from his splendid collection are well represented in this book and his patient research in tracing their history has proved invaluable. Others I must thank are Chris Taylor for giving me the benefit of his knowledge of passenger transport; Dennis and Billy O'Neill, willing helpers who have been more than generous in their support and encouragement; my cousin, Tommy Davies, who has gone out of his way to be helpful; all those who supplied the photographs and gave me their consent to reproduce them, and finally the media, especially the *South Wales Echo* and Frank Hennessy of CBC, who have brought the books to the notice of a wide public. I am deeply grateful.

Bryn Awel,
Buttrills Road,
Barry, South Glamorgan   STEWART WILLIAMS

2 *(Opposite)* How many notice the sculptured bust of Minerva which surmounts the south from of the Central Library in the Hayes? The original building, designed by James, Seward an Thomas, was opened in July 1882. An open market existed on the Hayes island from 1890 until i removal to Mill Lane on 29 December 1952. This view was taken some time after 1898 when th underground lavatories were built

City, Suburbs and Docks

3 Queen Street in the 1890s. The *Victoria Hotel (left),* on the corner of Frederick Street, was demolished *c.*1937

4 Looking down High Street towards the Castle, *c.*1894

5 Womanby Street, March 1891. Trinity English Congregational Chapel, on the left next to the *Horse & Groom,* had been transferred to New Trinity, Cowbridge Road, two years before

6 Evans Court in the shadow of the Castle walls in North Street (later Kingsway) was in a state of dilapidation in 1890. St John's Church gives geographical meaning to this south facing view

7/8 *(Above)* This bird's eye view taken in 1906 from the Castle Clock Tower shows how narrow Duke Street was before congestion was relieved following its widening in 1923; *(below)* the partially hidden Castle, with Keep just visible, are seen in this across-the-rooftops view dating from the same period

9   The North Gateway of Cardiff Castle, rebuilt in 1922 on excavated Roman foundations

10   The First World War was just a year away when this tranquil scene of the fountain in Sophia Gardens was taken

11 This superb view taken in 1912 from the roof of the *Great Western Hotel* looking south shows the Glamorganshire Canal (with a fine collection of barges below the bridge), East and West Canal Wharves and the entrance to Custom House Street

12 This is how Mill Lane looked in 1939 with the Glamorganshire Canal on the right, Stuart Hall, Salvation Army HQ, in the middle distance, and John Bull Stores on the corner of Bridge Street

13 Crossing Duke Street with a pram was not impossible in the mid-1930s when this was taken

14 These houses in Paradise Place on the southern side of Queen Street were 'built in 1835, demolished in 1910, and photographed on 16 February 1910' as the writing on the end house confirms

15 Park House on the south-east corner of Park Place was owned by Mr Bradley, a solicitor, who gave land adjacent to it for Cardiff's first theatre, the Theatre Royal, which was opened in 1826 and destroyed by fire in 1877. The *Park Hotel* now occupies this site

16/17 The last houses occupied as private residences in Queen Street, between Dumfries Place and Windsor Place, were demolished in December 1925; *(below)* this is how they looked in March 1912 when they housed families of some substance

18 The Taff Vale *(in foreground)* and Rhymney Railway bridges in Newport Road were landmarks to generations of Cardiffians, but recent road improvements have swept away the buildings in this 1890s view and replaced the old bridges with a new structure

19 The Dock and Railway Strike of 1890 brought out the crowds to watch a procession to the Colonial Hall, New Street. These spectators gathered at the junction of Bute Street and Custom House Street. Note the original *Golden Cross* in the background

20 The horse and cart, bicycle and pram were the only traffic hazards in Clifton Street, Roath, in 1909

21 Newport Road looking west towards town, 1909. The entrance to Howard Gardens is on the left

22 A single-deck tram (necessary because of the low bridges in Salisbury Road) turns out of Crwys Road into Woodville Road, *c.*1910

23 City Road, looking north, *c.*1912

24 Whitchurch Road, 1918

25 Horse and hand carts straddle the tram lines in Albany Road, *c*.1910

26 This view of Whitchurch Village was taken from the church tower in 1905

27 Whitchurch Library, built with financial assistance from Andrew Carnegie, and Velindre
Road, *c.*1912

28   Tyn-y-parc Road, Whitchurch, 1910

29   Gwyn's Cottage, 1919. This dwelling stood about 50 yards to the west side of Merthyr Road almost opposite the present Rich's Road

30 Station Road, Llanishen, 1908

31 Roath Market, Constellation Street, *c.*1894

32   Chancery Lane, Canton, decorated for the Coronation of King George VI in 1937

33   This was Cowbridge Road, Canton, in 1909

34/35 Victoria Park, some 20 acres in extent, was opened on 16 June 1897 to serve the residents of Canton. Among its attractions, apart from immaculately tended flower beds, shrubs, trees and grassland, was a small menagerie—the monkey house is shown above—and a lake in which 'Billy the seal' performed antics for the delight of children of all ages. The iron railings (*below*) were removed in the scrap drive at the start of the Second World War

36 The legendary 'Billy', now part of Cardiff folk-lore, was in fact a female grey seal. She came from off the coast of Ireland in one of Neale and West's trawlers in 1912 and remained a favourite until her death in April 1939 when she was presented to the Dept. of Zoology at the National Museum of Wales. Her skeleton is in the osteological collection

37 Visible on the right of this 1925 photograph is the First World War tank which together with guns were removed from Victoria Park to help the war effort for a second time in 1939

Victoria Park, Cardiff 426

38/39 The 11-acre Thompson's Park in Canton developed out of an act of generosity by Charles Thompson in April 1891 when he opened to the public the gardens then existing on part of Cae-Syr-Dafydd, together with part of the playing field. In 1895 he enlarged the gardens and had them professionally landscaped. Mr Thompson conveyed the freehold of the land to the Corporation in 1912 and continued to manage the Park on an annual basis, appointing and paying the staff. He gave six months' notice of termination in 1923 at the expiry of which in April 1924 control passed completely to the local authority

40 The sand playground at Thompson's Park held special appeal for youngsters who rarely visited the seaside when these photographs were taken 80 years ago.

41 The ornamental lake and fountain and well-tended flower beds have always delighted visitors to Thompson's Park

42 The bandstand at Splott Park, c.1911. This 17-acre open space was a gift from Lord Tredegar

43 An Edwardian summer's day in Roath Park Recreation Ground, c.1905, before Ty-draw Road was built-up

44 St Fagans Castle was built by Dr John Gibbon in the latter part of the 16th century. It eventually passed to the Plymouth family who retained it from 1730 to 1946 when the Earl of Plymouth generously offered the Castle and its 18 acres of gardens and grounds to the National Museum of Wales as a Welsh Folk Museum which was opened to the public on 1 July 1948

45 Thatched cottages at St Fagans, *c.*1920

46   This aerial view of Llandaff from the south was taken in July 1936

47   Llandaff Cathedral School occupies this large mansion originally known as Llandaff Court. An impressive Georgian building, it was built between 1744 and 1751. In 1869 it was acquired by the See for use as an episcopal palace and was renamed Llys Esgob. The house was requisitioned during the Second World War; afterwards, in 1958, it was converted to form a new home for the Cathedral School

Front View of Bishops Palace and Chapel, Llandaff.
(Cathedral in distance.) No. 113.

48 Old Cottages in High Street, Llandaff, *c*.1890

49 High Street, Llandaff, *c*.1910. Shops and offices now occupy the site screened by hoardings.
Visible is the old village school, now demolished

50 The Green, Llandaff, 1914. The City Cross was restored and reset in 1897

51 Cardiff Road, Llandaff, *c.*1920. The Probate Registry, on the left, a splendid example of Victorian architecture, was built in 1857. It was designed by John Prichard

52 Horse chestnut trees are still an attractive feature of St Fagans village as they were seventy years ago when these children sat under the spreading arms of this fine specimen

53 Pontcanna Cottages, opposite Pontcanna Street, were demolished in 1897-98, to make way for grander houses in Cathedral Road. Teilo Street now runs down the right hand side of the line of buildings

54 The transition from wooden to iron ships, from sail to steam, was just beginning when this nostalgic scene was captured at Cardiff Docks in 1890.

55 The expressions on the faces of these Cardiff Channel Pilots reflect confidence. It was taken in 1880 and the donor's grandfather, Charlie Arch, is standing extreme right

56 A typical ship's crew caught by the camera in Cardiff Docks, 1910

57 Five men were killed and three injured when the steam boiler of the Cardiff tugboat the *Rifleman* blew up at Pier Head on 9 March 1886. The explosion rocked the town and according to an eye-witness 'one man was thrown high into the air and over the Bute Dock Offices'. Flying debris was scattered over a wide area

58 Adelaide Street, Docks, *c.*1908

59 The Glamorganshire Canal has gone—and the *Torbay Hotel*—but they were very much part of the docks scene when this party was photographed aboard the sailing ship *Winnie* in the early years of this century

60 The drained bed of the remaining part of the Glamorganshire Canal following the collapse of the sea lock gates on the night of 5-6 December 1951

61 This fire float, built by Merryweather and supplied in November 1912, was berthed on the sea lock of the Glamorganshire Canal. Her beam had been reduced so that she could pass through the locks of the Canal on the northern side of Queen Street and also through 'the tunnel'

62 Fletcher's Timber Wharf, Roath Dock, August 1965

63/64 These aerial views of Cardiff Docks were taken in the 1930s. They show *(above)* Roath Dock and Basin, and *(below)* the Queen Alexandra Dock which was opened in July 1907

Trade and Industry

65 This section of Queen Street, seen in 1905, occupied part of the site on which the Carlton Restaurant was later built

66 The Carlton in its hey-day, 1922. Note the 'dare-devil' window cleaners using the glass canopy to rest their ladder

Carlton Restaurant and Principality Buildings, Queen Street, Cardiff.

WYMAN & SONS, LTD.

67 Edwin Poole's chemist shop, 71 Broadway, Roath, in 1906. Poole was in business for about 20 years

68 'The Whartons', employees of James Howell, about to set off on their annual outing, 1913. Their rugby club used the *Blue Anchor* (see No. 80) and filled the bar with their cups and plaques

69 Edwards's bakery business grew with the development of the Ely housing estate. Their bakehouse was situated behind the former Avenue cinema in Llanwern Road. Frank, the youngest of four Edwards brothers, is seen here with his delivery van in the 1920s

70 In the early days of electric lighting the Brewer brothers ran a flourishing little business in Quay Street

71 Walter Pratten outside his boot store in Bridge Street, *c*.1910

72 David Jones' tailor's shop on the corner of Albany Road and Diana Street, 1911. He was in business for 20 years

73 This ingenious GPO float was entered in a 1935 carnival procession. The vehicle was a Morris Commer

74 A 1909 post card advertising Roath Steam Laundry which was situated on the corner of Blenheim Road and Marlborough Road. In later years the premises were occupied by United Welsh Mills

75/76 The section of Cowbridge Road between Green Street and Lower Cathedral Road was known as Westbourne Place when these photographs of the *Westgate Hotel* were taken. *(Above)* Decorated for a Royal occasion, probably the Coronation of King George V in June 1911; *(below)* in 1933, shortly before rebuilding

77 The *Pembroke Castle* in Louisa Street, Butetown, c.1915. Walter Mitchell was the licensee until it closed in the early 1930s

78 The *Three Horse Shoes* photographed in 1900. One of Cardiff's oldest inns (records date back to 1798 but it was in existence earlier), it was situated midway along the western side of High Street. Demolished in 1913

79 *Carpenters Arms,* Newport Road, Rumney, 1916

80 The *Blue Anchor* in Wharton Street, 1900. This old pub was demolished *c*.1929 and is now part of James Howell's store

81 Dowlais Wharf men, Roath Dock, whose job was to unload iron-ore vessels for BSC East Moors Works. Taken about 1957

82 Dowlais Wharf, East Moors, dockworkers at Roath Dock, *c.*1958

83 Fifteen-ton electric crane at work in Hill's Dry Dock, *c.*1930

84 Six-ton hydraulic grabbing cranes at GKN's Dowlais Iron Ore Wharf, Roath Dock, 1942

85/86 By 1920 the serious decline in the coal trade of Cardiff Docks prompted vigorous effort by the Council to attract the import of general cargo to replace the lost coal exports. Fruit (being unloaded here in the 1940s), vegetables and cattle from the Commonwealth and the Mediterranean slightly improved a depressed situation

Religion and Education

87 Mary Slamin, one of the flower strewers from St Peter's Corpus Christi procession, 1925

88 'The Squires of Saint Columba' outside St Alban's, Splott, *c*.1935

89 Mount Hermon Primitive Methodist Chapel, Pearl Street, 1895. From 1916-17 it became the Salvation Army Splott Bridge Citadel

90 St Agnes Anglican Church, Bertram Street, *c.*1887

91 Ebenezer Baptist Chapel, Pearl Street, 1905

SCHOOL ANNIVERSARY WHIT SUNDAY

92 Moorland Road Presbyterian Forward Movement Hall, 1905. Opposite is the eastern end of Habershon Street

93 St Martin's Church, Albany Road, in the 1920s

94 The Mayoress (Mrs S. A. Brain) laying the foundation stone of St Martin's Church on 16 December 1899. In the group are the Bishop of Llandaff, Lord Tredegar, and the Mayor (Councillor Brain)

95 Roath Road Wesleyan Methodist Church on the corner of City Road, 1910. It was destroyed by enemy action during the Second World War

96 St Mary's Church, St Fagans, dates from the 12th and 13th centuries. It is a stone building in the Norman and Decorated styles of architecture

97 The Boys' Brigade 'on parade' for the visit of King Edward VII and Queen Alexandra to Cardiff in July 1907

98 Scouts from St Peter's, Roath, on a visit to Rome in 1939

99 With the horse brake acting as a makeshift grandstand members of the Mothers' Meeting from the Mission Hall on the corner of Harriet Street and Cairns Street, Cathays, pose for the photographer before setting off on their annual outing in 1912

100 David Evans, caretaker at Cardiff Central Library from 1890-1905, resplendent in full uniform with medals proudly displayed

101 Cardiff Intermediate School for Girls, The Parade, 1910

102 Generations of Cardiff youngsters aspiring to business careers received their education at Clark's College in Newport Road. View taken in 1913. The building was recently demolished

103 Adamsdown Schools, 1906

104 Corpus Christi procession, Lady
Mary School, 1966

105 Grangetown Board School, *c.*1900

106 Pageantry from pupils at St John's School in Queen Street, 1935

107 Marlborough Road School, 1921-22

108 St Peter's School, *c*.1922-23

109 Kitchener Road Infants' School, 1925

110 Kitchener Road School, Canton, 1933

111 Form IIA, St Illtyd's College, 1930-31. The master is the late Matthew Fennel of Rumney; to his left is Illtyd Turnbull, youngest brother of Maurice the pre-war Glamorgan cricket captain and test selector. Geoff Dart, South Glamorgan County Librarian, is third from right, sitting, in second row

112 Staff and girl pupils of Cleves College, Newport Road, *c*.1931

113   Herbert Thompson Infants' School, c.1930

114   Herbert Thompson Infants' School Band, c.1931

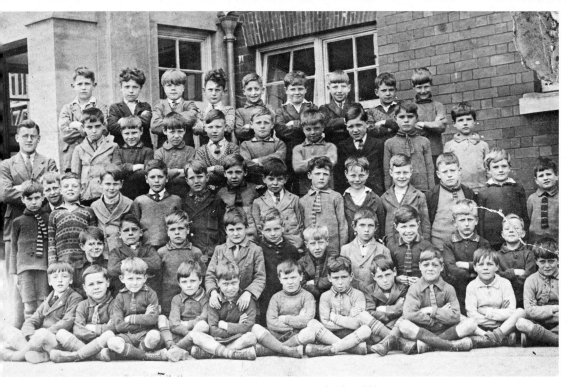

115   Herbert Thompson School, Ely, 1933

116   Standard 1A, Herbert Thompson School, Ely, 1938

117 Maindy Infants' School, c.1930

118 Standard 1, St Cuthbert's School, 1944

119 Form 3A, Severn Road School, 1952

120 Severn Road School, Canton, 1958

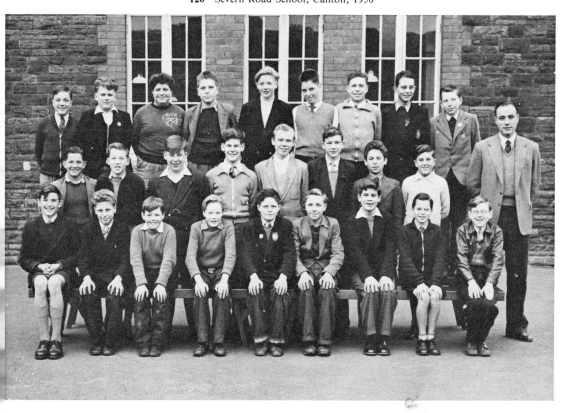

121 Moorland Road and Albany Road Girls' Schools on holiday at Porthcawl Camp, January 1951. Second from the right in the back row is Shirley Bassey who has since blossomed into an international show business personality. The donor of the photograph, Mrs A. Stubbs (née Wilson), now living in Dover, is fourth from the left, back row

122   Grange National School, 1948

123   Windsor-Clive, Ely, schoolgirls at Porthcawl Camp, 1952

124/125 De la Salle School in Richmond Crescent, Roath, now demolished to make way for flats, is a Preparatory School for St Illtyd's College. These groups date from 1961 *(above)* and 1966 *(below)*. The school moved to a new building at Rumney adjacent to the new St Illtyd's College in 1967

126 *(Opposite)* Jim Sullivan 'a legend in his life-time' was born at Splott and played rugby for Cardiff at 16. I June 1921, soon after his 17th birthday, he went north to join rugby league club Wigan. Between 1921 and 194 Jim scored an incredible 2,959 goals, 96 tries to make a total of 6,206 points. He played in 25 Test matches fc England and countless international games for Wales at Rugby League. In northern circles he is regarded as th greatest rugby player of all time

To Joe
from Jim
Wish All the Best

127 The Corsi brothers—Jack, Joe, Louis, Angelo and Rigo—have been described as 'one of the finest footballing families Wales has produced'. Born in Adamsdown, where their father had a grocery shop, and educated at St David's School, their outstanding talent soon attracted Rugby League interest and with the exception of Rigo (who stayed home and played for Cardiff under the captaincy of Danny Davies) they went North and collected many top honours during the 1920s with Rochdale, Oldham and York. Angelo, the sole survivor of this remarkable Cardiff—Italian family, stayed with York for seven seasons and in his best season scored 32 tries. The five Corsi brothers served in the First World War. Angelo *(left)* also served in the RAF 1940-45

128 Angelo and Jack Corsi *(extreme left and second left, middle row),* members of York Rugby League team, winners for the first time of the Yorkshire Rugby League Cup, December 1922

129 *(Left to right)* Jack, Louis and Joe Corsi at Grove Park, London, in 1916

130 Rochdale Hornets, 1921, winners of the Rugby League Cup. Joe *(fourth left, standing)* and Louis Corsi *(extreme right, standing)* were outstanding members of this team

131 Cardiff RFC, 1898-99. Famous names include Gwyn Nicholls (captain), H. V. P. Huzzey (vice-captain), H. B. Winfield and W. O'Neill

132 Famous Cardiff rugby personalities in this group include Wilf Wooller, Jack Bowcott, Duncan Brown, Tom Holley, Ted Spillane, Danny Davies, Jack Powell and Arthur Cornish. The occasion was a 'past and present' game in May 1946, the last of the Cardiff benefit games to raise cash for local hospitals before the setting up of the National Health Service

133 GKN rugby XV and officials, winners of the Mallett Cup, 1952. Captain was Stan O'Brien

134   Whitchurch RFC, 1910

135 St David's RFC, 1911-12, Mallett Cup and Welsh League Shield Winners. They are wearing a set of presentation jerseys donated by Edward Curran. Captain was Peter Conway, vice-captain D. O'Brien

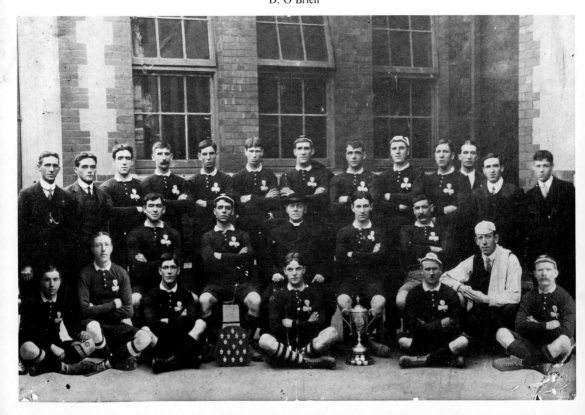

136   Team and officials of St Peter's CYMS rugby club about to depart on their 1956 Irish tour

137   Schoolboy rugby champions in 1934 were Highfields & Hawthorn (First Division) and St Patrick's (Second Division) seen here receiving the Cardiff Schools Shields from Lascelles Carr

138 Opening of the John Cory Workmen's Institute in Wellington Street, Canton, by Sir Clifford Cory M.P. on 3 July 1909

139 The billiards room at the Cory Institute

140   Gladstone Swimming Club, *c*.1906

141   St Cadoc's Athletic Club, Canton, 1935

New Pavilion, Cardiff Arms Park. No. 658.

142 Erected in 1904 for the joint use of Cardiff cricket and rugby football clubs, the New Pavilion at Cardiff Arms Park, with its striking twin turrets, served for 30 years before it was dismantled in the 1930s. It stood in the south-west corner of the cricket field

143 Cardiff East Cricket Club, Champions of Cardiff & District Cricket League, 1912

144 This 1922 photograph shows the American Roller Rink after it had been dismantled and re-erected in Mill Road, Ely, where it served as a concrete castings depot for Cardiff Corporation. It originally stood in Westgate Street adjacent to the GPO and was opened in 1908

145 Police on duty at the American Roller Rink during a strike in 1911 when the Rink was at the height of its popularity

146 Splott Park Bowling Green, *c*.1911. Note the tide-fields in the background

147 Bowling Green, Grange Gardens, 1913

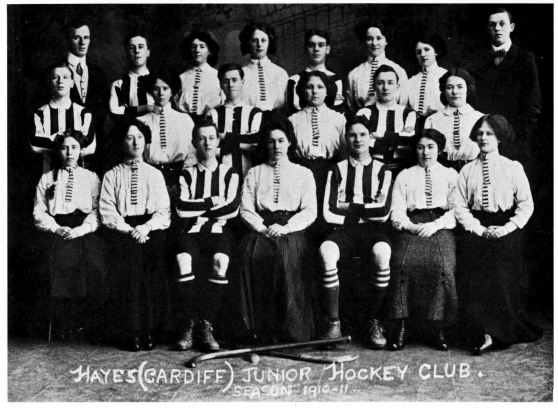

148 Not surprisingly these smartly turned-out young men and women were employed by David Morgan Ltd., the Cardiff store

149 St Illtyd's College Junior cricket XI, 1937. On the extreme left, back row, is Dannie Abse

150 Grangetown has always produced first-class baseballers

151 Herbert Thompson School baseball team, 1936. Third Division champions and cup winners, 1936; Second Division champions and cup runners-up, 1937. Harry Frost (captain) is wearing a Cardiff Boys' rugby cap

152 This 1908-09 Cardiff baseball team, one of the earliest, was captained by Welsh international D. Davies

153 Splott U.S. baseball team, 1920s

154 Manager Cyril Spiers had just joined Cardiff City when this team group was taken in 1939. City were in the Third Division (South) and prominent players include *(back row)* Billy Baker, Arthur Granville, Bill Fielding, Jim Kelso; *(middle row)* Bill Cardhill, George Balisom; *(front row)* Jimmy Collins, George Walton, Reggie Pugh

7216   CARDIFF CITY A.F.C., 1913—14.   PUBLISHED BY IMPERIAL PRINT CO., CARDIFF.

TOP ROW: K. McKENZIE.   G. WEST.   J. EVANS.   J. KNEESHAW.   P. CASSIDY.   J. STEPHENSON.   E. MILFORD.   W. DAVIDSON.   T. W. WITTS.   T. H. ROBERTSON.
CENTRE ROW: T. DONCASTER.   J. K. BENNETT.   A. HOLT.   H. FEATHERSTONE.   J. H. BURTON.   H. HARVEY.   W. HARDY.   H. WARD.   R. LEAH.   J. CLARKE.
BOTTOM ROW: G. BURTON.   H. TRACEY.   W. DEVLIN.   H. KEGGANS.   W. B. GAUGHAN.   J. HENDERSON.   F. C. KEENOR.

155 Billy Hardy and Fred Keenor, later to become household names, were starting their soccer careers when this team group was taken

156 Walter Robbins played for Ely United before joining Cardiff City in 1928. He first appeared for Wales in 1930 in the famous 'unknowns' team who held Scotland to a 1-1 draw at Hampden Park, and went on to win a further nine caps. Scored five goals from the left wing at Ninian Park in City's record 9-2 win over Thames United. Joined West Bromwich Albion in 1932. In 1946 Robbins returned to Cardiff as coach moving to Swansea when Billy McCandless left City in 1948

157 Riverside Albion FC, 1918, at Ninian Park. On the far right in bowler hat is Bartley Wilson whose long and distinguished association with Cardiff City is well known. Next to him is Fred Evans who played for City and Newport County

158 Park Villa FC, 1923

159 Heath FC, 1913-14, with Gladstone School in the background

160 Cathays United, 1919

161 Cardiff Dockers FC, 1947-48. Joint holders of Donovan Cup, semi-finalists Newlands Cup. Captain was Freddy Parsons

162 Roath Road Brotherhood FC, 1928

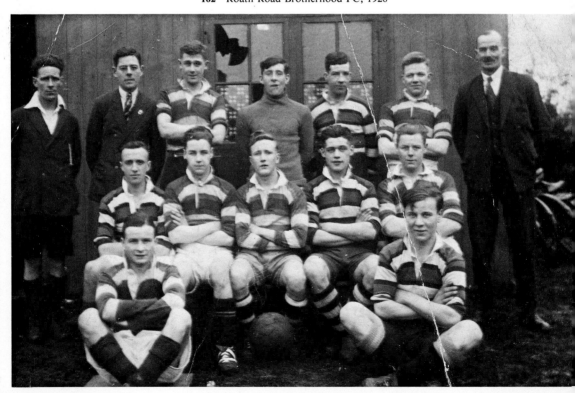

CARDIFF SCHOOLS' FOOTBALL LEAGUE · 52nd SEASON · 1947-1948

Mr. W. B. Richards, Mr. J. E. Jenkins, W. Jones, A. Regan, E. Willis, D. Cross, R. Farrell, Mr. G. Evans, Mr. J. Cross, Mr. T. Stevens
(Ex-Chairman)   (Trainer)   (Asst. Secretary)   (Trainer)   (Trainer)

Mr J. Sullivan, Mr. C. M. Mullins, G. Nash, C. Crocker, A. Harrington, R. Searle, H. Pritchard, Mr. C. Dunn, Mr. E. N. Walbrook
(Vice-Chairman)   (Chairman)   (Hon. Secretary)   (Hon. Treasurer)
                        Thomas   E. Westlake

163 Cardiff Schools' Football League, 52nd Season, 1947-48

164 Moorland Road School 'soccer nursery', 1966

165 A charity soccer match between Rumney & St Mellons British Legion and an 'All Stars' side was played on Boxing Day 1958. Well-known faces in the front row include Ken Devonshire, Billy James, Billy Lewis and Roy Phillips

166 Cardiff Cosmos FC, 1954-55. First Division Champions in Cardiff & District League. Record: played 24, won 20, drew 3, lost 1. Goals for 102, against 37. The captain *(centre)* was Jim Pleass, also well-known as a Glamorgan cricketer

167 Johnny Coombes, the Cardiff-born middle-weight, 1964. He was Welsh ABA Schools Champion, Junior British ABA Champion and British Army Cadet Champion, before turning professional

168 John Hill distinguished himself playing centre-forward for St Francis School, Ely. Between 1935-38 he scored 70 goals. John also played for Cardiff Boys

169 Doug Kestrell in September 1935, the year he narrowly lost on points to featherweight champion of the world Freddie Miller

'The fighting Kestrells of Cardiff'—Alby, Frank and Doug—were household names in the 1920s and 30s meeting many of the big names in boxing and deservedly winning a reputation as one of the most famous of Wales's fighting families. Their real name, Cheverton, was changed to Kestrell as it was considered more suitable for professional use. Alby and Frank are now dead, but Doug is alive and well and lives in Ely. Doug won the first 36 of his 235 fights and of the total he fought as a pro he won 180 and drew 22. His opponents included world champions Freddie Miller and Jackie Wilson, Bert Kirby, Dick Corbett, Dave Crowley, Harry Mizler and Arthur Danahar

170 Doug Kestrell *(right)* at the weigh-in for his fight with Arthur Danahar in November 1938

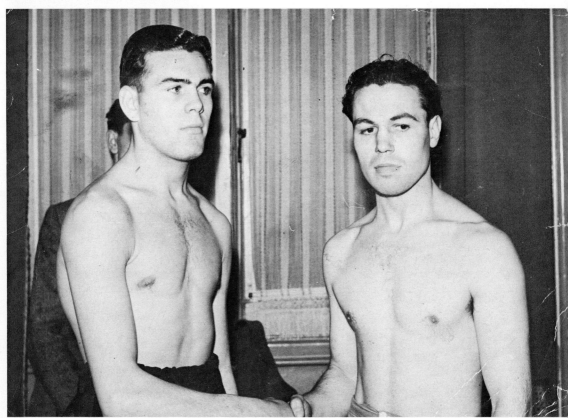

171 Alby and Doug watched by Frank sparring in the ring behind the *Cross Inn*, Gabalfa, scene of many a fine scrap

172 *(Left to right)* Alby, Doug and Frank Kestrell, big names in pre-war Welsh boxing

173 Cardiff boxer Fred Perry seen in his team uniform for the Olympic Games at Amsterdam in 1928 when he reached the semi-finals before being narrowly beaten by Dutchman Van Klaveren who went on to win the gold medal. A stylish fighter, Fred was Welsh ABA champion at feather-weight in 1924/26/27/28/29 before taking the lightweight title in 1932, the year he collected the title of All Irish Champion of the World at the Tailtean Games in Dublin. Fred remained an amateur and carved out a successful business career in outdoor advertising, his Cardiff-based business being well-known in South Wales. He died in January 1981

174 St David's Military Band, pre-First World War. Included are two men who later made their mark in industry, Edward Curran *(second left, middle row)* and his brother John Curran *(sixth left, middle row)*

175 This *c.*1920 dance orchestra, one of the earliest in Cardiff, played at various functions often in the Whitehall Rooms of the *Park Hotel*. The conductor was Archibald Griffiths and the drummer Eli Cook (donor's father) claimed to be the first dance drummer in the city

T. Jenkins. A. Harding. W. A. Morgan. F. Undry. R. Meluish. W. J. Goulden. A. France. W. Brookman. R. F. Stephens. A. France. C. Chapman.

A. C. Gedrych. V. Williams. J. D. Tobin. W. J. Quick. G. H. Jones. G. Morris. E. Davies. E. Slatter. G. Brooks. D. MacPherson. R. Dudridge. A. Streeter. A. Codd. C. Combs. J. H. Miller.

H. E. Gedrych. J. Webb. A. Western. H. Govier. A. Alridge. T. Brady. G. Coffee. W. J. Bonsall. W. Orchard. F. Lewis. J. Toogood. A. Bolton.

W. Gedrych. A. Tayler. J. H. Dixon. E. Collier. T. Hilliard. M. H. Ash, Rod. Roderick (Conductor). H. Jones (Sec). D. Lewis (Vice Chairman). F. May (Pianist). C. Ansell. F. Robbins. D. Jones (Deputy Conductor).

176   Canton Liberal Institute Male Voice Choir, 1922

177   The Curran Choral Society with their conductor, Wyndham Jones, during the 1939-45 war years when they gave numerous concerts in the city

Transport

178 The year is 1909 and a solid-tyred Dennis double-decker operated by the Cardiff Tramways Company trundles along Merthyr Road, Whitchurch. The service ran between town and Llandaff North via Church Road, the fare being 4d. The firm's premises were in Andrew Road, Llandaff North

179 A fine body of Riverside men prepare for a day's outing in a Cridland's charabanc, *c.*1925. The photograph was taken in Westgate Street

180   Liberty Motors Ltd., of 15 Picton Place, Canton, operated this Ensign 30-seater charabanc bought from Romilly Motors Ltd., for £1,400 in July, 1919. It could be converted into a lorry when required and was eventually sold in 1929. According to Chris Taylor not many of these Ensign commercials were made as the firm was principally a car manufacturer

181   Liberty were still operating in 1949-50, under the umbrella of Red & White Services. This Albion coach in cream and green livery was used for tours and express services

182/183 Charabanc outings were highly popular in the 1920s. *(Above)* 'regulars' of the *Grosvenor*, South Park Road, about to depart for Cheltenham in August, 1920; *(below)* Cathays Terrace Methodists out for a more comfortable ride on pneumatic tyres, *c.*1929. Tom Coakley (later a city councillor) is second from the left

184 AEC Regent 56-seater double-decker on the Roath Dock, Splott—Clive Street, Grangetown service, c.1950. This was before road improvements changed the lay-out of the Monument in St Mary Street

185 Thomson House, home of the *Western Mail* and *South Wales Echo,* now occupies this site which in 1949 was used as a terminus by 'bus operators. The vehicle is a Leyland 56-seater

186 E. T. Willows, 'Britain's foremost airship pioneer', was born in Cardiff in 1886. He devoted his life to this controversial type of aircraft and was killed n a balloon accident at Kempston, Bedford, on 3 August 1926. In the last year of the Great War he set up as a balloon manufacturer in Cardiff. His factory was the former American Roller Rink in Westgate Street where this photograph was taken. At one time Willows employed 150 staff, but the business folded soon after the cessation of hostilities

187 TVR staff at Grangetown demonstrated pride and patience when they picked out the name of their station in white marble chippings, *c.*1909

188 The original Taff Vale Railway Station in Queen Street was replaced by a new building in 1887. This photograph was taken in 1907

189 Cardiff Railway locomotive No.5 was built in 1898 and became GWR No. 1338 in 1923 following the absorption of the Cardiff Company. It is seen here in Pengam marshalling yards in the 1930s. Man in the middle is the late E. Mathews who worked 48 years for GWR. He died in January this year aged 99

190 Road haulage contractor E. Price of New Road, Rumney, had been in business for two years when this was taken in 1934. The firm has expanded over the years and still operates from New Road

191 Lance-Corporal Samuel Vickery was awarded the Victoria Cross in May 1898 'for conspicuous bravery during operations in the Sudan'. This consisted of 'rescuing a wounded comrade under a heavy fire' and 'killing three of the enemy who attacked him when separated from his company in the Waran Valley'. Vickery lived for many years in 33 Romilly Crescent, Canton

192 The news caused great excitement in
Cardiff and Mafeking Night became an
established occasion. During the war against the
Boers Mafeking was defended by a few soldiers
and civilians under Col. Baden-Powell from
October 1899 to May 1900

193 Duke Street decorated for the visit of King Edward VII and Queen Alexandra to open the
Alexandra Dock in July 1907. Taken from above the Duke Street Arcade looking towards
Kingsway and Queen Street

194 When King Edward VII and Queen Alexandra visited Cardiff to open the Alexandra Dock in July 1907 the decorations were described as being 'of an extent and character seldom equalled'. This was the scene in Bute Place

195 The Cubitt family lived for over 30 years in Rumney House on Rumney Hill

196 Contingent of the 7th (Cyclists) Battalion of the Welsh Regiment prior to leaving Cardiff for Scotland. On the right is Captain Hammond, the officer in command

197 Territorial display at Cardiff by Welsh Regiment cyclists

198/199 Albany Road School was commandeered for use as a military hospital during the First World War. *(Above)* wounded soldiers arriving, watched by a crowd of patriotic Cardiffians; *(below)* these patients could manage to smile despite their wounds

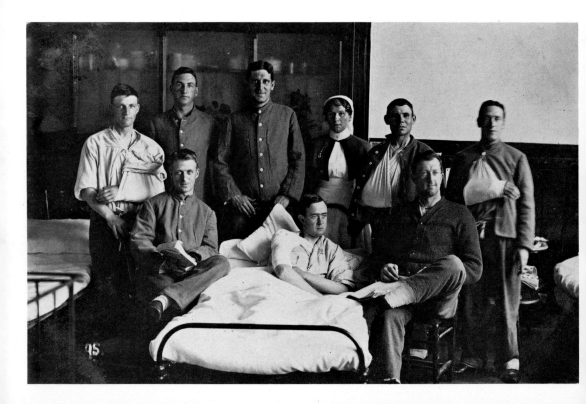

200   Some of the patients at Albany Road School proudly display their 'Kaiser Bill' souvenir

201   Medical and nursing staff at Albany Road School military hospital

202   This was typical of the thousands of food parcels sent to Welsh prisoners of war in Germany in the First World War. Each cost five shillings and was paid for by a fund raised by the Lady Mayoress of Cardiff (Mrs J. T. Richards)

203   Men of the Welsh Casualty Clearing Hospital marching to the General Railway Station in 1916 where they were inspected by Brigadier-General Curll

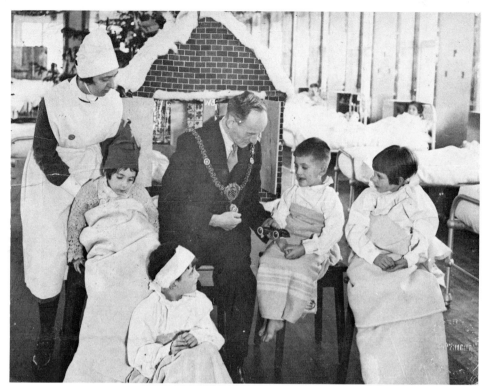

204 Llandough Hospital had just been opened when six-year-old Roy Edwards received his present from the Lord Mayor (Alderman A. E. Gough) on Christmas Day 1933

205 The flags in Daniel Street, Cathays, were out for First World War hero Sgt. (later Lt.) Frank Barter who won the Victoria Cross

206/207   King George VI and Queen Elizabeth visited Cardiff on 14 July 1937. *(Above)* The King inspects a Guard of Honour of Welsh Guards outside the City Hall; *(below)* the King and Queen chat to ex-servicemen in Cathays Park

208/209 Many will remember the air raid shelters in the Castle walls. They were reached by wooden gangways in Castle Street (just visible in the above view) and Kingsway. V. C. Hardacre remembers a sunny June afternoon in 1940 when the air raid sirens gave warning of an attack and shoppers streamed into the shelters leaving the streets empty. Fortunately it was a false alarm, but the shelters proved their usefulness

210 War seemed imminent when this photograph was taken in 1938 and hurried preparations were in hand to provide shelter against air attacks. Ironically the site of these activities was adjacent to the Temple of Peace in Cathays Park

211 Cardiff City Special Constabulary, 'A' Parade, 1940. Chief Inspector C. A. S. Hawkins and Commandant T. R. Morgan are in the centre of the front row

212   Supervisory staff of Cardiff Corporation Public Works Department, April 1929

213   A. Arnall Bloxham, the well-known Cardiff hypnotherapist, is in the centre of the front row with Mrs Bloxham on his left, in this RNVR group. The occasion was a Christmas Party on HMS Cambria at Cardiff Docks in the early 1950s

SHIP AHOY!

ON VIEW, ANCIENT ORIGINAL

CONVICT SHIP

"SUCCESS," from Australia.

ON TOUR NOW 14 YEARS.

(Late at Thames Embankment, London.)

WEST BUTE DRY DOCK, CARDIFF,

UNTIL NOVEMBER 19th, then other Ports.

Raised from the Bottom of Sydney Harbour!
A Nautical Curiosity! 72 Cells! Wax Models!
Museum! Armoury! "Compulsory Bath,"
and Prison Chapel! The Sight of a lifetime.

Ex-COUNCILLOR HARVIE (of Melbourne)

Lectures to seated audiences, 4 and 8 p.m.

GUIDES AT WORK ALL DAY.

From Deck to Deck descend conveniently!

Hours, 10 to 10. Sundays, 2 to 6.

A Historic Relic! A Treat!

VISITED BY ROYALTY, LORD ROBERTS, LORD
ROSEBERY, and many other distinguished visitors.

Just 6d. No Extras. Children Half-price.

214 Edwardian Cardiff provided many attractions but few as curious as the visit of the convict ship *Success* to Bute West Dock. This is the souvenir card issued on the occasion

THE CONVICT SHIP, Visited by Royalty. 10.
Contains 78 Ancient Cells, Life-like Figures and Prison Relics.

215 The convict ship *Success* at Bute West Dock (see 214)

216 Hovercraft trials at Cardiff Docks in the 1960s. Subsequently a service was operated between Penarth and Weston by P. & A. Campbell

P.S. CARDIFF QUEEN AND WESTLAND HOVERCRAFT S.R.N.7.

217 Eight-year-old Eileen O'Neill helping a charity by selling shamrocks on St Patrick's Day, 1917. The Cardiff-Irish community held an annual procession through the main streets of the city until the Second World War

218 A *c*.1959 outing organised by regulars and friends of the *Red Lion*, Ely